House of Blues Learn to Play

BEGINNER
ELECTRIC GUITAR

W9-CZK-882

Method by John McCarthy

Written and Adapted by Steve Gorenberg

Supervising Editor: Joe Palombo
Layout, Graphics and Design: Steve Gorenberg
Photography: Joe Palombo, Scott Sawala
Audio Engineer: Joe Cuzino

Copy Editors and Proofreaders:
Alex Palombo, Cathy McCarthy, Irene Villaverde

Cover Art Direction and Design:
Sarah Dekin and Jennifer Pienkoski

Produced by The Rock House Method®
© 2006 Fred Russell Publishing, LLC   All Rights Reserved

House of Blues Photos © 2005 House of Blues   All Rights Reserved

Table of Contents

John McCarthy
author of
The Rock House Method

John is a virtuoso guitarist who has worked with some of the industry's most legendary musicians. He has the ability to break down, teach and communicate music in a manner that motivates and inspires others to achieve their dreams of playing an instrument.

John is the creator of **The Rock House Method**®, the world's leading musical instruction method. Over his 20 year career, he has produced and/or appeared in more than 100 instructional products. Millions of people around the world have learned to play music using John's easy to follow, accelerated program.

As a guitarist and songwriter, John blends together a unique style of Rock, Metal, Funk and Blues in a collage of melodic compositions, jam-packed with masterful guitar techniques. His sound has been described as a combination of vintage guitar rock with a progressive, gritty edge that is perfectly suited for today's audiences.

Throughout his career, John has recorded and performed with renowned musicians like Doug Wimbish, Grammy winner Leo Nocentelli, Rock & Roll Hall of Famer Bernie Worrell, David Ellefson, Will Calhoun, Jordan Giangreco and Alex Bach. He has also shared the stage with Blue Oyster Cult, Kansas, Al Dimeola and Dee Snyder.

For more information on John, his music and his instructional products, visit www.rockhousemethod.com.

CREATING MUSICIANS
ONE LESSON AT A TIME

Introduction

Welcome to **The Rock House Method**® system of learning. You are joining millions of aspiring musicians around the world who use our easy-to-understand methods for learning to play music.

Unlike conventional learning programs, **The Rock House Method**® is a four-part teaching system that employs DVD, CD and 24/7 online lesson support along with this book to give you a variety of sources to assure a complete learning experience. Each product can be used individually or together. The DVD that comes with this book matches the curriculum exactly, providing you with a live instructor for visual reference. You can pause, rewind, or fast forward any lesson. In addition, the DVD contains some valuable extras like sections on changing your strings, guitar care, and an interactive chord library. The CD that we've included lets you take your lessons with you anywhere you go.

How to use the lesson support site

Every Rock House product offers FREE membership to our interactive Lesson Support site. Use the member number included with your book to register. You will find it on the sleeve that contains your DVD and CD. Go to www.hob.com, click the icon on their home page and you will be taken to The Rock House Method Lesson Support site. Once registered, you will use this fully interactive site along with your product to enhance your learning experience, expand your knowledge, link with instructors, and connect with a community of people around the world who are learning to play music using **The Rock House Method**®. There are sections that directly correspond to this product within the *Additional Information* and *Backing Tracks* sections. There are also a variety of other tools you can utilize such as *Ask The Teacher, Quizzes, Reference Material, Definitions, Forums, Live Chats, Guitar Professor* and much more.

Icon Key

Throughout this book, you'll periodically notice the following icons. They indicate when there are additional learning tools available on our support website for the section you're working on. When you see an icon in the book, visit the member section of www.rockhousemethod.com for musical backing tracks, additional information and learning utilities.

Backing Track

Many of the exercises in this book are intended to be played along with bass and drum rhythm tracks. This icon indicates that there is a backing track available on our support site for that particular lesson. You can download these tracks and create a CD to practice with.

Additional Information

The question mark icon indicates there is more information for that section available on the website. It can be theory, more playing examples, or tips.

Metronome

Metronome icons are placed next to the examples that we recommend you practice using a metronome. You can download a free, adjustable metronome from the support site.

Tablature

This icon indicates that there is additional guitar tablature available on the website that corresponds to the lesson. There is also an extensive database of tab music online that is updated regularly.

Tuner

Also found on the website is free tuner software which you can download to help you tune your instrument.

CHAPTER 1
Parts of the Guitar

The guitar is divided into three main sections: the body, the neck and the headstock. The guitar's input jack will be located on the side or front of the body. The assembly that anchors the strings to the body is called the bridge. The saddles hold the strings properly in place; the height of each string (or *action*) can be adjusted with the saddle. Mounted to the body behind the strings are the pickups. A pickup functions like the guitar's microphone; it picks up the vibrations of the strings and converts them to a signal that travels through the guitar cord to the amplifier. Also located on the front of the body are the volume and tone knobs and the pickup selector switch or *toggle switch*. Strap buttons are located on both sides of the body where a guitar strap can be attached. The front face of the neck is called the fretboard (or *fingerboard*). The metal bars going across the fretboard are called frets. The dots are position markers (or *fret markers*) for visual reference to help you gauge where you are on the neck while playing. The nut is the string guide that holds the strings in place where the neck meets the headstock. The headstock contains the machine heads (also referred to as *tuners*); the machine heads are used to tune the strings by tightening or loosening them.

Holding the Guitar

Throughout this book, we will refer to the picking hand as your right hand, and the hand fretting the notes as your left hand. If you are left handed and playing a left handed guitar, just make the necessary adjustments as you follow along (read "right hand" to mean your left hand and vice versa).

The photos below show the proper way to hold a guitar. Rest the body of the guitar on your right leg when sitting. When standing, attach a guitar strap to the strap buttons and wear the strap over your left shoulder. Locate the input jack on your guitar. Before you plug in, turn the volume down on the guitar; the amplifier should be *off*. Plug the cord into the guitar and the amplifier, then turn the amp on and bring up the volume.

Rest the guitar on your right leg when seated.

When standing, the guitar strap goes over your left shoulder.

Be sure the amplifier is turned off before you plug in.

Insert the cord all the way into the input jack.

Holding the Pick

Hold the pick between the index finger and thumb of your right hand. Leave just the tip pointing out, perpendicular to your thumb. Your thumb and finger should be placed in the center of the pick, grasping it firmly to give you good control. Leave your hand open (don't make a fist), and let the rest of your fingers hang loosely.

Grasp the pick between your index finger and thumb.

Leave your hand open and your other fingers loose.

To properly position the pick, center the pick on your index finger (Fig. 1) and bring your thumb down on top of it (Fig. 2). Pinch your thumb and finger together and leave just the tip of the pick showing (Fig. 3).

Fig. 1

Fig. 2

Fig. 3

Right Hand Position

Place your right arm on the very top of the guitar and let it drape down almost parallel to the bridge (Fig. 4). Leave part of your hand or fingers touching the guitar's body and keep them anchored to the guitar (Fig. 5). This will help give your picking hand a reference point.

Fig. 4

Fig. 5

Left Hand Position

Hold your left hand out in front of you with your wrist straight (Fig. 6). Curl your fingers in and just naturally bring your hand back to the neck of the guitar (Figs. 7 & 8). Try not to bend or contort your wrist. Your fingers should stay curled inward; most of the time only your fingertips will touch the strings when playing. The first joint of your thumb should be in the middle of the back of the neck (Fig. 9). Try to avoid touching the neck with any other part of your hand. Make sure you have the proper right and left hand positions down so that when we progress, you'll have no problems.

Fig. 6

Fig. 7

Fig. 8

Fig. 9

Tuning

Each of the six strings on a guitar is tuned to and named after a different note (*pitch*). The thinnest or 1st string is referred to as the highest string because it is the *highest sounding* note. The thickest or 6th string is referred to as the lowest string because it is the *lowest sounding* note. Memorize the names of the open strings. These notes form the basis for finding any other notes on the guitar.

Names of the Open Strings

6th string	5th string	4th string	3rd string	2nd string	Ist string
E	A	D	G	B	E

6th string (thickest)
lowest sounding string

Ist string (thinnest)
highest sounding string

Tune your guitar using the machine heads on the headstock. Turn the machine heads a little bit at a time while plucking the string and listening to the change in pitch. Tighten the string to raise the pitch. Loosen the string to lower the pitch. Be careful not to accidentally break a string by tightening it too much or too quickly.

The easiest way to tune a guitar is to use an electronic tuner. There are many different kinds available that are fairly inexpensive. You can also download the free online tuner from www.rockhousemethod.com.

Reading a Chord Chart

A chord is a group of notes played together. A chord chart (*chord diagram*) is a graphic representation of part of the fretboard (as if you stood the guitar up from floor to ceiling and looked directly at the front of the neck). The vertical lines represent the strings; the horizontal lines represent the frets.

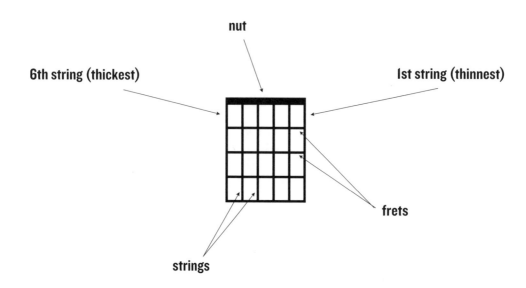

Chord diagrams show which notes to play and which strings they are played on. The solid black dots within the graph represent fretted notes and show you where your fingers should go. Each of these dots will have a number directly below it, underneath the diagram. These numbers indicate which left hand finger to fret the note with (1 = index, 2 = middle, 3 = ring, 4 = pinky). The 0s at the bottom of the diagram show which strings are played open (strummed with no left hand fingers touching them).

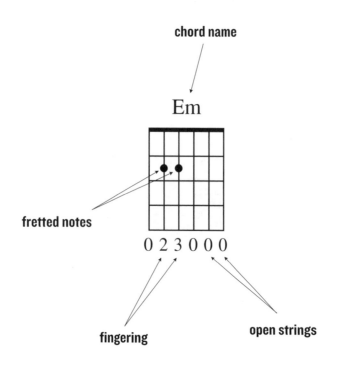

Minor Open Chords

Our first two chords are two of the easiest and most commonly used chords in rock and blues, A minor and E minor. In the Am chord diagram, the "x" at the 6th string means that string is not played (either muted or not strummed). For each chord, the first photo shows what the chord looks like from the front. The second photo is from the player's perspective.

Am

x 0 2 3 1 0

Em

0 2 3 0 0 0

Remember to keep your thumb firmly anchored against the back of the neck. Your fingers should be curled inward toward the fretboard and only the tips of your fingers should be touching the strings. Don't grab the neck with your whole hand; no other parts of your fingers or hand should be touching the neck or any of the other strings. Place your fingertips just to the left of (behind) the fret, pressing the strings inward toward the neck.

Let's start off with a simple downstrum. Fret the Am chord with your left hand. Starting from the 5th string, lightly drag the pick downward across the strings in a smooth motion. Now switch to the Em chord and strum downward from the 6th (thickest) string. The strumming motion should come from your elbow. When strumming chords, pivot from your elbow and keep your wrist straight. When playing single notes, use more wrist.

One of the hardest things for a beginner to conquer is the ability to play a clean, fully sustained chord without buzzing strings, muted or dead notes. Make sure your left hand is fretting the proper notes and your fingers aren't accidentally touching any of the other strings. Pick each string individually with your right hand, one note at a time. If any of the open strings are deadened or muted, try *slightly* adjusting your fingers. If any of the fretted notes are buzzing, you probably aren't pressing down hard enough with your fingers. It will be difficult at first and might hurt a little, but don't get discouraged. With time and practice, you'll build up callosses on your fingertips. Before you know it, playing chords will be second nature, and your fingers will hardly feel it at all.

Strumming Rhythm

Once you have the chords sounding clean and the strumming motion down, the next step is to learn how to change chords quickly and cleanly. Focus on where each finger needs to move for the next chord. Sometimes one or more of your fingers will be able to stay in the same place. Avoid taking your hand completely off the neck. Instead, try to move your whole hand as little as possible and make smaller finger adjustments to change from one chord to the next. When you can change from chord to chord seamlessly, you'll be able to play complete songs.

The following is an example of a *chord progression* and is written on a musical *staff*. A staff is the group of horizontal lines on which music is written. The chord names above the staff show which chord to play, and a *rhythm slash* simply means to strum the chord. In this chord progression, strum each chord twice, using all downstrums. This example also uses *repeat signs* (play through the progression and repeat it again). Listen and play along with the backing track to hear how it should sound. Keep practicing and try to change chords in time without stalling or missing a beat. Count along out loud with each strum, in time and on the beat. Start out slowly if you need to and gradually get it up to speed.

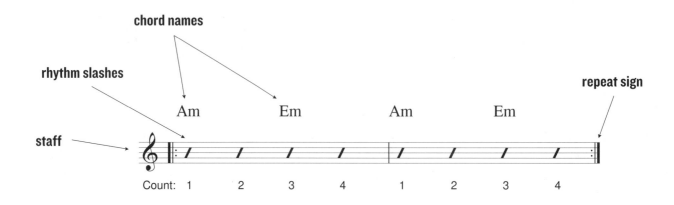

Chapter 1 Overview

1) **Parts of the guitar:**
   Body - pickups, bridge, volume and tone controls
   Neck - frets, fret markers
   Headstock - machine heads

2) **Hold the pick with your thumb and index finger. Keep your picking hand open and try to anchor it to the guitar.**

3) **Keep your wrist straight on your fretting hand. Place your thumb in the middle of the back of the neck.**

4) **Names of the open strings:**

6th string (thickest)	5th string	4th string	3rd string	2nd string	1st string (thinnest)
E	**A**	**D**	**G**	**B**	**E**

5) **Use your fingertips when fretting notes. Place your finger close to the fret to get the best sound and playing ease.**

6) **When strumming, pivot your arm from the elbow.**

Quick Tip!

CHOOSE YOUR TEACHER WISELY

Finding a good guitar teacher is essential, especially for beginners. Playing well and teaching well are separate skills. Just because someone can play guitar doesn't automatically mean they have the proper skills to teach guitar. Before you commit to a teacher, you may want to ask for a trial lesson to make sure you're happy with the communication skills and the teaching method the instructor provides. If you're not learning from someone who knows how to teach, you may have a difficult time.

CHAPTER 2

Major Open Chords

Now it's time to learn the seven major open chords. Major chords have a happy or bright sound, whereas the minor chords have a sad or melancholy type of sound.

In the **A** chord diagram, the slur going across the notes means you should *barre* (bar) those notes. A barre is executed by placing one finger flat across more than one string. Pick each note of the chord individually to make sure you're applying enough pressure with your finger. Notice that the 6th and 1st strings are not strummed.

A

x 0 1 1 1 x

B

x x 2 3 4 1

C

x 3 2 0 1 0

D

x 0 0 1 3 2

E

0 2 3 1 0 0

The hardest open (or *1st position*) chord to play is the F chord. This chord is difficult because you need to barre the highest two strings with your first finger and put your 2nd and 3rd fingers down straight. If you tilt your 1st finger barre to the left side, it makes it easier to fret the other notes properly. Pick each note out individually to make sure the chord sounds clean and that you're playing it correctly. Memorize all of the major open chords. Practice playing them and changing from chord to chord efficiently.

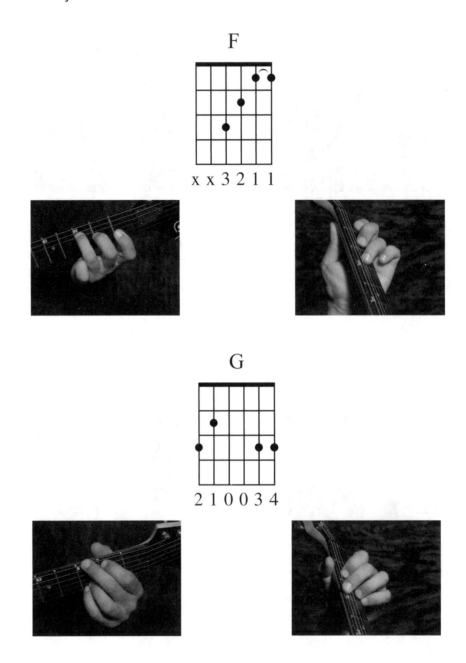

Quick Tip!

ALWAYS TUNE YOUR GUITAR

Make sure your guitar is in tune every time you play it. You could be playing all of the right notes, but they'll sound incorrect if you haven't tuned up. Even if only one string is slightly out of tune, the simplest of chords will sound bad. It's a good idea to stop and check your tuning from time to time while practicing.

Major Open Chord Strumming Pattern

This example is played in an *eighth note* rhythm; strum twice for each beat. Each chord is downstrummed eight times. Listen to the backing track and practice changing chords cleanly and in time. You can download all of these backing tracks from the Rock House Lesson Support site and practice along with them.

Count: 1 and 2 and 3 and 4 and etc...

Measures and Timing

You don't need to read traditional music notation in order to play guitar, but it's helpful to understand a little bit about the concept of rhythm and timing. In most popular rock and blues, music is divided into *measures* of 4 beats. When a band counts off "One, two, three, four" at the beginning of a song, it represents one complete measure of music. Different types of notes are held for different durations within a measure. For example, a *quarter note* gets one beat because a quarter note is held for one quarter of a measure.

Whole notes are held for 4 beats.
Count: 1   2   3   4

Half notes are held for 2 beats.
Count: 1   2   3   4

Quarter notes are held for 1 beat.
Count: 1   2   3   4

Eighth notes are held for 1/2 beat.
Count: 1 and 2 and 3 and 4 and

Sixteenth notes are held for 1/4 beat.
Count: 1 e and a 2 e and a 3 e and a 4 e and a

19

A *tie* is a curved line connecting one note to the next. If two notes are tied, strike only the first one and let it ring out through the duration of the second note (or 'tied' note).

Count: 1   (2)   3   (4)   1   2)   3   (4)

A *dot* after a note increases its value by another 1/2 of its original value. In the following example the half notes are dotted, so they are held for 3 beats.

Count: 1   (2   3)   4   1   (2   3)   4

Picking Exercise

Here's an alternate picking exercise to help coordinate your right hand. Instead of strumming the chords, you might pick the notes of a chord out individually and let them ring out together. The following symbols indicate whether a note is picked in an up or a down direction:

⊓ - **downpick (pick down toward the floor)**

∨ - **uppick (pick up toward the ceiling)**

Fret an open D chord and hold the chord shape with your left hand while picking out the individual notes in the order indicated below. This picking pattern (indicated by which number string you pick) is 4 - 1 - 3 - 1 - 2 - 1. Recite the string number while you pick each one to help memorize the order. Use a down-up-down-up alternate picking pattern. Notice that the 1st string is always uppicked, while the other strings are all downpicked. Try to hold one of your right hand fingers on the body of the guitar to help give you added support and control. Practice playing in a steady, even rhythm, in time with a metronome.

D

x 0 0 1 3 2

string number:	4	1	3	1	2	1
picking direction:	⊓	∨	⊓	∨	⊓	∨

Alternate Strumming

This progression combines both major and minor chords. When changing chords, look for common notes from one chord to the next one; don't move any fingers that can remain on the same notes. You can modify the fingering of the Em chord and fret the notes using your 1st and 2nd fingers. This will allow you to leave at least one finger stationary, making it easier to switch chords

Up until now, we've only been using downstrums. Here's a popular strumming rhythm that combines both up and downstrumming. Play the chords above the staff in the rhythm and strumming pattern indicated. When alternate strumming, keep your arm relaxed and don't grip the pick too tightly. Stay nice and loose so that your strumming sounds smooth, not stiff or forced.

This exercise utilizes a strumming technique that we call a *ghost strum*. A ghost strum occurs when you move the pick over the strings without actually striking them. This allows you to keep your arm moving in a constant down-up-down motion, keeping your playing fluid and in time. The strumming symbols in parentheses indicate where ghost strums occur.

If you're having trouble changing from chord to chord smoothly, isolate the change and just practice going back and forth between those two chords. With practice, you'll build finger memory and your fingers will instinctively know where to go. Play this rhythm along with the backing track and get the changes, the feel, and the strumming motion down.

Tablature Explanation

Tablature (or *tab*) is a number system for reading notes on the neck of a guitar. It does not require you to have knowledge of standard music notation. This system was designed specifically for the guitar. Most music for guitar is available in tab. Tablature is a crucial and essential part of your guitar playing career.

The six lines of the tablature staff represent each of the six strings. The top line is the thinnest (highest pitched) string. The bottom line is the thickest (lowest pitched) string. The lines in between are the 2nd through 5th strings. The numbers placed directly on these lines show you the fret number to play the note at. At the bottom, underneath the staff, is a series of numbers. These numbers show you which left hand fingers you should use to fret the notes.

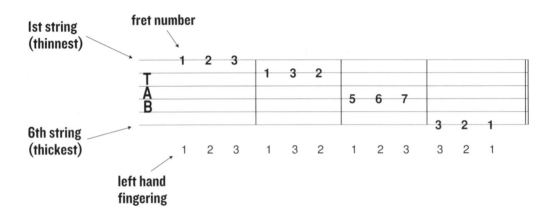

Chords can also be written in tab. If there are several numbers stacked together in a column, those notes should be played or strummed at the same time. Here are the chords you've already learned with the tablature written out underneath each diagram. Since the fingerings are shown on the chord diagrams, we won't bother to repeat them underneath the tab.

A

x 0 1 1 1 x

```
T   2
A   2
    2
B   0
```

B

x x 2 3 4 1

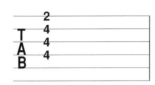

```
T   2
A   4
    4
B   4
```

C

x 3 2 0 1 0

```
T   0
A   1
    0
B   2
    3
```

D

x 0 0 1 3 2

```
T   2
A   3
    2
B   0
    0
```

E

0 2 3 1 0 0

```
T   0
A   0
    1
B   2
    2
    0
```

F

x x 3 2 1 1

```
T   1
A   1
    2
B   3
```

G

2 1 0 0 3 4

```
T   3
A   3
    0
B   0
    2
    3
```

Finger Flexing

This is a finger exercise in tablature that will build coordination and strengthen your left hand. Fret each note individually, using one finger at a time. Play each measure four times, then proceed to the next measure without pausing. This will help build endurance. Use alternate picking, and practice this exercise using the metronome for timing and control.

Quick Tip!

MAKE SURE YOUR GUITAR IS SET UP PROPERLY

Beginners don't usually realize that their new guitar may need to be set up for it to play comfortably. A proper set up will ensure that the strings are at the correct height. If they're too high off the neck, it will be harder to press the strings down. You'll also want to check the neck adjustment to be sure your guitar neck has the proper curve. Even right out of the box, new guitars need adjusting. This oversight can cause many beginners to give up in frustration before giving it a fair chance on a properly adjusted instrument.

Chapter 2 Overview

1) Major chords have a happy or bright sound; minor chords have a
   sad or melancholy sound.

2) To barre, hold down more than one note with one finger.

3) Music is broken down into small sections called measures. Most music
   will have three or four beats per measure.

4) Alternate picking is consistent down-up-down picking.

5) A ghost strum occurs when you move your arm over the strings,
   but your pick doesn't strike the strings.

6) The tablature staff consists of six horizontal lines representing the strings
   on the guitar. The numbers placed on these lines represent the frets you play
   the notes on.

CHAPTER 3
Basic Blues

The following is a basic blues riff in the key of A. This riff is made up of two note chords shown on the tab staff. The chord names above the staff are there as a reference to show you what the basic harmony is while you play along.

This riff should sound very familiar - it's used more than any other blues progression. Plenty of rock and blues classics are played entirely with this one riff repeated over and over. It is made up of 12 measures (or *bars*) of music called the *12-bar blues*.

Fingering: 1   1 3   3 1   1 3   3   etc...

Blues is played with a *shuffle feel*, also called a triplet feel. This example was written in eighth notes, and the second eighth note of each beat should lag a little. This is referred to as triplet feel because the beat is actually divided by thirds, counted as if there were three eighth notes per beat instead of two. The first part of the beat gets 2/3 of a beat, and the second part only gets 1/3.

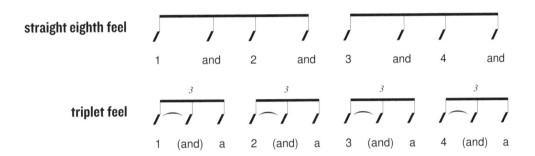

Shuffle feel is a much easier concept to understand by hearing it. Listen to the backing track, count along and try to get the triplet feel in your head. Also, check out almost any blues standard, slow or fast, and you'll probably recognize a shuffle feel being used.

This 12-bar blues riff is also an example of a **I - IV - V** (one - four - five) chord progression. The roman numerals refer to the steps of the scale, relative to what key the music is in. This blues riff is in the key of A, so the A chord is the **I** chord (also called the *tonic*). The D chord is the **IV** chord (also called the *subdominant*) because in the key of A, D is the fourth step of the scale. Finally, the **V** chord (or *dominant*) is the E chord, because E is the fifth step of the scale in the key of A.

The I - IV - V chord progression is the most common progression used in rock or blues. It's the foundation that all rock and blues was built on and has evolved from. There are many variations, but songs such as "Johnny B. Goode," "You Really Got Me," "Rock and Roll," "I Love Rock and Roll" and "Sympathy for the Devil" are all based on the I - IV - V.

Quick Tip!

TEST YOUR MEMORY

The easiest way to memorize a piece is through repetition. The more you repeat each part, the easier it will be to hear in your head. You may find it easier to memorize something by breaking it into small sections. Be sure to have the first few bits down before moving on and memorization should begin to happen naturally.

Picking Chord Progression

Let's go through a progression that picks out the chords and combines individual picking with strumming. This is a popular two chord progression using the D and G major chords. When changing from chord to chord, notice the third finger on your left hand can stay on the same note. Leave this finger stationary when switching and concentrate on moving the other fingers. Once you've got the picking pattern and chord change down, practice playing along with the backing track and staying in time.

Quick Tip!

PLAY SLOWLY AT FIRST

When learning something new, don't start out trying to play it as fast as possible. Take things slowly at first; play slow enough so you don't keep making mistakes. Build your speed over time. A great tool for learning to build speed gradually is a metronome. This is a device that clicks at an adjustable rate that you set. A metronome allows you to gauge your progress each day. By playing along with the click, you learn to play in time with other instruments.

Half Steps & Whole Steps

The distance in pitch between any two musical notes is called an *interval*. An interval is how much higher or lower one note sounds from another, or the space in between the notes. The smallest interval on the guitar is from a fretted note to the fret next to it on the same string. This distance is called a *half step*. Twice the distance, or the distance of two frets, is called a *whole step*.

The musical alphabet uses the letters **A** through **G**. The distance from one letter or note to the next is usually a whole step (two frets), with two exceptions: there is only a half step between the notes **B** and **C** and between the notes **E** and **F**.

whole step	half step	whole step	whole step	half step	whole step	whole step	
A	B	C	D	E	F	G	A

After counting up from **A** to **G**, we get to a higher sounding **A** and can continue to count up higher through the alphabet again from there. The distance from that first **A** to the next **A** (higher or lower) is called an *octave*.

The Chromatic Scale

Counting up or down the musical alphabet in half steps (or frets) is called a chromatic scale. The regular letters of the alphabet are called *natural notes*. Where there is a whole step between two natural notes, the note that falls in between them is a *sharp* (♯) or *flat* (♭) note. The ♯ next to a note makes the note a half step higher. The ♭ lowers the note a half step. For example, the note in between A and B can be called either an A♯ or a B♭, since it's actually the same note with two different names. Whether you call a note sharp or flat depends on what key you're playing in or what the context is. The half steps that occur between B and C and between E and F (where there aren't other notes between them), are referred to as *natural half steps*. If you memorize where these two natural half steps occur, you can use that knowledge to find any note on the guitar. Just start with any open string and count up in half steps.

natural half steps

A   A♯/B♭   B   C   C♯/D♭   D   D♯/E♭   E   F   F♯/G♭   G   G♯/A♭   A

Ascending Chromatic Scale

The following is an exercise that goes up through the chromatic scale in the 1st position of the guitar. Notice that when playing up the scale there are only 12 different notes until you reach an octave and start over with the same letters. These are the 12 notes that make up all music. The name of each note is written above the tab staff.

Descending Chromatic Scale

Here's the first position chromatic scale in reverse, descending from highest to lowest note, using all flats. Practice both the ascending and descending chromatic scales using the metronome to build up speed and coordination.

Minor Open Chords

Now let's play the rest of the minor open (or 1st position) chords. Notice that the Bm and Cm chords both have the exact same fingering. To go from Bm to Cm, simply slide your hand up the neck one fret. The Fm and Gm chords contain a first finger barre and also use identical fingerings; Fm is played at the 1st fret, and Gm is played one whole step higher at the 3rd fret.

Bm

x x 3 4 2 1

Bm

```
    2
T   3
A   4
B   4
```

Cm

3fr

x x 3 4 2 1

Cm

```
    3
T   4
A   5
B   5
```

Dm

x 0 0 2 3 1

Dm

```
      1
   T  3
   A  2
   B  0
      0
```

Fm

x x 3 1 1 1

Fm

```
      1
   T  1
   A  1
   B  3
```

Gm

3fr

x x 3 1 1 1

Gm

```
      3
   T  3
   A  3
   B  5
```

Minor Chord Progression

Here's a popular strumming rhythm that combines both up and downstrumming, as well as major and minor chords. The rhythm used is an example of *syncopation*. You're playing a syncopated rhythm if there's one or more strums off the beat, or on the *upbeat* instead of the downbeat. The strum on beat 2 1/2 is tied to beat 3, so you don't strum directly on beat 3. Keep your arm moving in a consistent down-up-down-up motion, with a ghost strum occurring on beat 3. Once you have the chord changes and strumming fluent, download the backing track from the Rock House Lesson Support site and practice playing along with the bass and drums.

Quick Tip!

DEVELOP GOOD PRACTICE HABITS

Knowing how to practice efficiently will accelerate your progress. Set aside a certain amount of time for practicing and have a routine that reviews all of the techniques you know. Create your own exercises that target weaknesses in your playing. It's important to experiment and get creative as well; try things fast or slow, light or hard, soft or loud.

Chapter 3 Overview

1) 12-bar blues is an example of a I - IV - V chord progression.

2) A shuffle beat is an uneven rhythm often used in blues.

3) To move a note up or down the neck one half step, just move it one fret. A whole step requires moving the note two frets.

4) The chromatic scale consists of the 12 notes that make up all music:
   A - A♯ - B - C - C♯ - D - D♯ - E - F - F♯ - G - G♯

5) To find any note on the guitar, start with the name of an open string. Then, using the chromatic scale notes, move up the neck one fret at a time until you find your note.

In the studio with Will Calhoun, Leo Nocentelli, Doug Wimbish and the staff at Horizon Recording Studio.

John rocks The Roseland Ballroom in New York City.

Demonstrating his lighting fast techniques at Music Player Live.

CHAPTER 4

Power Chords

Power chords are simple two note chords that are used extensively in rock and metal. Power chords sound their fullest and heaviest when played with distortion. Below are two power chords shown at the 1st fret; both are played using just the first and third fingers.

F5

1 3 x x x x

F5

Bb5

x 1 3 x x x

Bb5

The two notes that make up power chords (also referred to as *five* chords) are called the *root note* and the *fifth*. The root note of the F5 power chord is F, the note that gives the chord its name. The other note is a C, which is the fifth note up the musical alphabet from the root note (F-G-A-B-C). These power chords are actually abbreviated versions of regular major and minor chords. Major and minor chords are made up of root notes, thirds and fifths. The third is the note which determines whether a chord is major or minor. Since power chords contain no thirds, they are neither major nor minor. Because of this, power chords can be an ideal choice for many different keys and styles.

Power chords are *moveable* chords; if you move the same fingering to another fret, the name of the chord changes. This is called *transposing* the chord. Notice that the lowest note of each power chord is the root note. Using the musical alphabet and the chromatic scale, you can transpose the power chords to any chord in the scale. For example, if you take the F5 chord and move it one whole step higher to the third fret, it will become a G5 power chord. The chart below shows the notes along the fifth and sixth strings up to the 12th fret. You can use this chart to transpose the F5 and B♭5 power chords to any other fret.

6th string notes (F5 chord)	E	F	F♯	G	G♯	A	A♯	B	C	C♯	D	D♯	E
fret number	Open	1	2	3	4	5	6	7	8	9	10	11	12
5th string notes (B♭5 chord)	A	B♭	B	C	C♯	D	D♯	E	F	F♯	G	G♯	A

Power Chord Progression

Here's a popular progression using all power chords. Use only your first and third fingers to fret each chord and practice moving smoothly from chord to chord. This exercise has been written in eighth notes, but you can experiment with the rhythm and strumming and come up with your own variations. Play along with the backing track and try it in different ways. Instead of eighth notes, try playing sixteenth notes, quarter notes or half notes. You can use alternate strumming, or try using all downstrums to create a chunkier, metal sound. As you progress, you'll notice that the way you attack or strum the strings will make a big difference in the overall sound.

Quick Tip!

EXPERIMENT AND CHALLENGE YOUR CREATIVE MIND

It's great to be able to play along with your favorite recordings note for note, but you can get even more out of practicing by analyzing and experimenting with them. Isolate your favorite riffs and sections and transpose them to other keys. Try playing them at different speeds using different techniques. Hear how the notes interact with the chord progressions and apply these ideas to different situations. All of this will help you to build a well rounded improvisational vocabulary.

The Minor Pentatonic Scale

Minor pentatonic scales are the most commonly used scales for playing rock and blues solos. The pentatonic is a five note scale, or an abbreviated version of the full natural minor scale. The word "pentatonic" comes from the greek words, "penta" (five) and "tonic" (the keynote).

Memorize and practice this scale; it's the one you'll use most often for playing melodies and leads. There are five different positions of this scale, each beginning on a different note of the scale. The first two positions are shown below. To the right of each tab staff is a scale diagram. These are similar to the chord diagrams we've previously used. A scale diagram shows you all the notes in the scale within a certain position on the neck. The stacked numbers below the diagram indicate the fingering for the notes on each string.

1st Position Am Pentatonic Scale

1st position

Fingering: 1 4 1 3 1 3 1 3 1 4 1 4

5fr

1 1 1 1 1 1
4 3 3 3 4 4

2nd Position Am Pentatonic Scale

2nd position

Fingering: 2 4 1 4 1 4 1 3 2 4 2 4

8fr

2 1 1 1 2 2
4 4 4 3 4 4

38

Triplet Lead Pattern

Here is the A minor pentatonic scale you've just learned played in groups of three notes, or triplets. Count "one - two - three, one - two - three" out loud while you play through this exercise to get the triplet feel in your head. This is a standard lead pattern exercise, designed to help you build coordination and learn how to begin using the minor pentatonics for playing leads. Use alternate picking and the metronome to start out slowly and get the rhythm. Gradually speed it up and before you know it, you'll be playing blazing rock and blues guitar solos.

Fingering: 1 4 1 4 1 3 1 3 1 3 1 3 1 3 1

3 1 3 1 3 1 3 1 4 1 4 1 4 1 4

Now let's play the same pattern in reverse, back down the scale in triplets. After you have the pattern memorized, try using it to practice the 2nd position minor pentatonic scale as well.

Fingering: 4 1 4 1 4 1 4 1 3 1 3 1 3 1 3

1 3 1 3 1 3 1 3 1 3 1 4 1 4 1

Barre Chords

Two very important chords are the F and Fm barre chords. These are full barre chords containing no open strings, so they are moveable chords. The lowest sounding note in the chord is the root note; you can transpose them to any fret using the chart located earlier in this section.

Full barre chords are especially difficult to play. For the F barre chord, you need to barre your 1st finger across all six strings, then add the other three notes as well. Pick out each note individually to make sure it sounds clean. Once you've got the F barre chord down, simply lift your second finger and you'll have the Fm barre chord.

F

1 3 4 2 1 1

F

Fm

1 3 4 1 1 1

Fm

Chapter 4 Overview

I) Power chords are two note chords made up of the root note and fifth scale tones.

2) The minor pentatonic scale is a five note scale used widely in rock and blues.

3) A triplet is a rhythmic pattern that groups three notes for each beat.

4) Barre chords are moveable chords. They can be transposed and played at any fret along the neck; the root note determines the name of the chord.

Recording session at Horizon Music Studio.

John onstage at Toad's Place in New Haven, CT

CHAPTER 5

Drop D Tuning

Drop D tuning refers to lowering the pitch of the 6th string from E to D. This gives the guitar a heavier, meaner sound. Drop D has been used for years in hard rock and heavy metal, so much so that many bands have written their entire catalogs in Drop D.

To tune your guitar to Drop D tuning, strike the open 4th string (D) and the open 6th string together and gradually lower the 6th string from E to D until the 4th and 6th strings sound "in tune" with each other. These two strings are now both tuned to D an octave apart from each other. You can check your tuning using the online tuner at www.rockhousemethod.com to make sure you've got it.

Drop D is extremely easy to play in because the 6th string power chords are now played with just one finger. Simply barre one finger across the lowest three strings at any fret. You can also play a D5 chord just by strumming the lowest 3 open strings.

D5	F5	G5
0 0 0 x x x	1 1 1 x x x	3 3 3 x x x

Here's a popular Drop D progression. Use all downstrums to give it that heavy metal feel. This rhythm is played as eighth notes, but notice that you strike the first two chords three times each, changing to the F5 chord on an upbeat. This gives the rhythm a syncopated, triplet feel. Try accenting the first strum of each new chord by strumming it a little harder. Play along with the backing track to help you feel where the accents should be.

```
      D5      F5      G5     D5      F5      G5     D5

T  ||:                       |                      |                      |                      :||
A  ||: 0 0 0  3 3 3  5 5  | 0 0 0  3 3 3  5 5  | 0 0 0 0 0 0 0 0  | 0 0 0 0 0 0 0 0  :||
B  || 0 0 0  3 3 3  5 5  | 0 0 0  3 3 3  5 5  | 0 0 0 0 0 0 0 0  | 0 0 0 0 0 0 0 0  ||
        0 0 0  3 3 3  5 5      0 0 0  3 3 3  5 5      0 0 0 0 0 0 0 0      0 0 0 0 0 0 0 0
accents: >        >       >    >        >       >
```

More Barre Chords

The Bb and Bbm barre chords are moveable chords with the root note of each chord on the 5th string. You can use the chart from the previous chapter to transpose these two chords to any other fret along the 5th string. For the Bb chord, you need to hold down the lowest note with your first finger, then barre across the other three strings with your third finger. For the Bbm chord, barre with your first finger and fret the other notes individually.

Bb

3fr

x 1 3 3 3 x

Bb

```
   3
T  3
A  3
B  1
```

Bbm

x 1 3 4 2 1

Bbm

```
   1
T  2
A  3
   3
B  1
```

Changing the Feel of a Song

By altering the strumming or picking pattern of a chord progression, you can dramatically change the style. In this section, we'll show you how to take a simple chord change and use it to play many different genres of music, all against the same bass and drum backing track. This demonstrates the power of the guitar and its ability to dictate the feel of the song. For each style, we'll use the same four barre chords. This progression is in the key of Am. Since all of the chords are moveable chords, you can transpose this entire progression to any other key.

Rock

This is a standard rock rhythm using the new progression. Play eighth notes using all downstrums.

Metal

Now play the same progression in sixteenth notes using alternate strumming to get that fast, heavy metal feel.

Reggae

Reggae uses all upstrokes. Following each upstrum of the pick, mute the strings with your picking hand in time and on the downbeat to give it that reggae feel.

Count: (1) and (2) and (3) and (4) and (etc.)

Ballad

This is a rock ballad picking pattern. Fret and hold each barre chord, and downpick the notes individually. Let the notes ring out together for the duration of each measure.

Quick Tip!

LEARN GRADUALLY AND HAVE REALISTIC GOALS

Don't try to play a lot of things you aren't ready for. Be realistic about your capabilities as a beginner and learn gradually. If you progress at a steady, methodical rate, your technique and control of the guitar will become solid as you advance. Strive to master each new technique, chord or scale before moving on to something else. Attempting things that you're not quite ready for can discourage you instead of inspire you to play.

Last Three Positions of the A Minor Pentatonic Scale

Here are the remaining positions of the minor pentatonic scales in the key of Am. Once you have all five positions mastered, you'll be able to play solos in any position on the neck. Use alternate picking when practicing these scales, and play through each scale position ascending and descending. Also try playing the three new positions using the triplet lead pattern from the last chapter.

3rd Position Am Pentatonic Scale

3rd position

4th Position Am Pentatonic Scale

4th position

5th Position Am Pentatonic Scale

5th position

Bending

Now let's learn some lead guitar techniques that will add expression to your playing. Bends are a very soulful way of creating emotion with the guitar, using flesh against steel to alter and control pitches. All guitarists have their own unique, signature way of bending notes.

The row of tab staffs below show bends using the 3rd, 4th or 1st fingers. The "B" above the staff indicates a bend, and the arrow with a "1" above it means to bend the note one whole step in pitch.

First try the 3rd finger bend. While fretting the note with your 3rd finger, keep your first two fingers down on the string behind it and push upward using all three fingers. This will give you added coordination and control. Use the same technique for the 4th finger bend, using all four fingers to bend the string upward. The 1st finger bend will probably be the hardest since you are only using one finger to bend the string. In some situations, you may even pull the string downward with your first finger to bend the note.

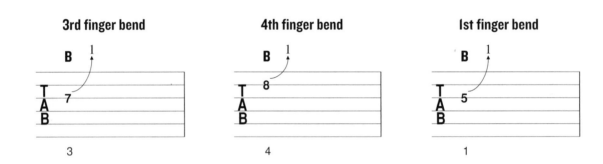

The following example shows what the bends might look like in context when playing a solo in the 1st position A minor pentatonic scale. Play through this exercise and start to get a feel for how to incorporate bends into your own riffs.

Hammer Ons and Pull Offs

Hammer ons and pull offs are two more widely used lead techniques. On the staffs below, you'll see a slur connecting one tab number to the next. This indicates that only the first tab number is picked; the second note is not struck. The "H" above the slur indicates a hammer on, and the "P" indicates a pull off.

To play a hammer on, pick the first note and then push down the next note using just your left hand finger (without picking it). Play through the series of hammer ons in the first meaure below to see how you can use these with the minor pentatonic scale.

Pull offs are the opposite of hammer ons. Pick the first note and pull or snap your finger off the string to the get the second note. Your first finger should already be in place, fretting the second note in advance.

The following exercise contains hammer ons and pull offs in combination. The slurs encompass three notes, so only pick the first one. Hammer on for the second note, then pull off to the third note. At the very end of the second measure, you'll see a squiggly line above the last note. This line indicates a technique known as vibrato. While sustaining the note, shake your finger slightly and "dig in" to the note to slightly vibrate the pitch and give it more expression.

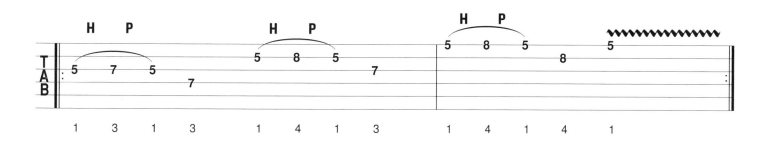

Complete Rhythm and Lead

For the last section of this program we'll use a complete rock rhythm and show you how to solo over it. First learn the rhythm part and play it along with the backing track. This is a rhythm based on barre chords in the key of A minor.

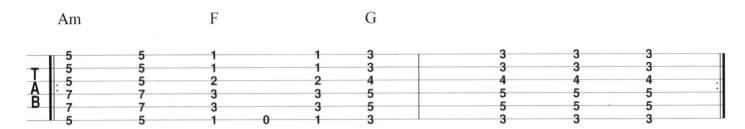

The following guitar solo incorporates all of the lead techniques and covers several positions of the minor pentatonic scale. After you've got this lead down, get creative and try improvising along with the backing track in every position of the A minor pentatonic, using bends, hammer ons and pull offs. You should now have a solid foundation for playing your own rock and blues solos.

Chapter 5 Overview

1) Drop **D** tuning is created by lowering the pitch of the 6th string from an "E" note to a "D" note.

2) When bending a note, use all of the left hand fingers before the note you are bending to help push up and control the note.

3) A hammer on is produced by pushing your finger down onto the neck with force; do not pick the note.

4) A pull off is produced by snapping or pulling your finger off from one note to the next without picking the second note.

Review Quiz

1) The names of the open strings, from lowest to highest pitched, are:
   A. B-E-G-A-D-E
   B. A-G-E-B-E-D
   C. E-A-D-G-B-E
   D. A-B-C-D-E-F

2) Quarter notes are held for
   A. one quarter of a beat
   B. four beats
   C. one beat
   D. ten years

3) The two major open chords that require you to barre more than one note are
   A. C and G
   B. A and F
   C. D and E
   D. 7 and 7

4) Minor pentatonic scales contain
   A. five different notes
   B. only minor notes
   C. one beat
   D. seven different notes

5) The note that gives a scale, key or chord its name is called the
   A. headstock
   B. first note
   C. root note
   D. shuffle note

6) How many different positions of the minor pentatonic scale are there?
   A. 6
   B. 3
   C. 5
   D. 7

7) Barre chords are
   A. moveable chords
   B. easy to play
   C. open string chords
   D. a hangover

8) Two frequently used lead techniques are
   A. tuning and strumming
   B. barre chords and open chords
   C. hammer ons and pull offs
   D. eighth notes and quarter notes

Electric Guitar Accessories

Strings & Picks

Strings and picks are both available in different gauges. Heavier gauge strings produce a thicker, fuller sound; lighter gauges are thinner, easier to bend, and great for soloing. There are many different types of picks in different thicknesses. A heavy pick may offer you more control for lead playing, but medium and light picks have a flexibility that's good for rhythm playing. A fingerpick is a type of ring that you wear on your thumb for downpicking, allowing all of your fingers to be available for more complex fingerpicking. When changing your strings, you'll probably want to use a string winder. A string winder is a simple gadget that fits right over the machine heads so that you can quickly wind or unwind a string.

String winder

Music Stands & Metronomes

As soon as you begin your first guitar lesson, you'll notice how important it is to have a music stand. Whenever you try to learn a new song from sheet music, or even go through a lesson in this book, you'll want to have the music right in front of you where it's close and easy to read. Don't try to balance a book on your lap or read it from the floor. If you're practicing scales and exercises or working out a difficult new guitar line, you can use a metronome to set a steady practice tempo and keep yourself in time. There are mechanical or electronic models, or you can download the free one from www.rockhousemethod.com and use your computer to keep time.

Electronic pocket metronome

Capos & Slides

A capo is a moveable clamp that attaches to the neck of the guitar and barres across all six strings. Whichever fret the capo is placed at can then be thought of as the nut; the capo transposes the entire guitar to that position, making it possible to play all of the open chords there. Many acoustic players prefer the full open chord sound and use capos almost exclusively. Capos are popular at the 1st, 2nd, 3rd, 5th and 7th frets, but you can place a capo anywhere at all on the neck. A capo at the 12th fret transposes the guitar one octave higher and gives it a bright, mandolin tone.

A capo is clamped to the neck.

Capo properly placed at the 2nd fret.

An essential element of the blues guitar sound is the slide. A slide is a sleeve (usually glass) that fits over the ring finger of your left hand. With a slide you can slide notes or chords in a steady, smooth motion, making the guitar "talk." Slide guitar is also very popular in many rock styles, and can be heard in songs like "Freebird" and "Bad to the Bone."

A slide can be worn on your ring finger.

Effects

Effects play an important role in every guitar player's arsenal. There are many different effects and different types of units available for you to experiment with while creating your own signature sounds. You can use foot pedals as well as rack mount effects units. Some basic effects that are useful are distortion, chorus, flangers and phasers, compressors, harmonizers and wah wah pedals.

With newer USB converters and software, you can also plug your guitar into a computer and play your way through cyberspace. Just connect right to your pc and you can get access to a whole arsenal of software featuring guitar effects, amp sounds, interactive lessons and virtual recording studios.

Tuners

An electronic tuner is a necessity for any gigging guitarist, and tuners have become so common that they're often included in other effects units. Tuners are also sometimes put right into a guitar's electronics. If you don't have a tuner, you can download the free online tuner at our support website.

Straps

Straps come in a variety of materials and styles. When picking out a strap, try to find one that's both comfortable and that looks good with your guitar. Also available are strap locks (locking buttons that will keep the strap secured to the guitar).

Cords

Investing a few dollars more to get a nice, heavy duty guitar cord is worthwhile. The cheaper ones don't last very long, while a professional quality cable can work perfectly for years. Some of the better cords even include a lifetime warranty. Cords also come in a variety of lengths, gauges and colors.

Cases & Stands

The two main types of guitar cases are hardshell cases and softshell cases. Hardshell cases are more expensive and have a sturdy construction designed for maximum protection during travel. A much lighter and smaller alternative to the traditional guitar case is a gig bag: a padded, zippered guitar glove that is carried over the shoulders like a backpack. Guitar stands are usually collapsible and easy to take with you, but you can also use one at home to keep your guitar on display when you're not practicing.

Make Your Own Tool Kit

Put together your own tool kit by keeping all of the important tools and spare parts you need in one place, like a small backpack or a compartment inside your guitar case. You should always have spare strings, a string winder, picks, batteries, and any small screwdrivers or wrenches that fit your guitar. You can purchase a multipurpose tool designed especially for guitarists (sort of like a pocket knife without the knife) that contains a few different types of screwdrivers and an assortment of allen wrenches. Some other good things to keep with you: wire cutters, fuses if your amp uses them, guitar polish and a soft cloth, music paper and pencil, and duct tape. You may also want to keep a small recording device handy to record your own musical ideas and use them to start writing your own songs.

our roots

House of Blues is a home for live music and southern-inspired cuisine in an environment celebrating the African American cultural contributions to blues music and folk art. In 1992, our company converted an historical house in Cambridge, Massachusetts into the original House of Blues®. The original House of Blues opened its doors on Thanksgiving Day, 1992 feeding the homeless before opening to the public. Our commitment to serving the community will always be a priority.

We now have the pleasure of bringing live music to 16 major markets in the U. S. and Canada through our 10 club and 19 arena and amphitheatre venues. Come share the House of Blues experience. Get intimate with your favorite band in our Music Hall or enjoy soulful sounds and eats at our popular weekend Gospel Brunch. Savor down home, southern inspired cooking in the restaurant. Be a VIP for an exclusive night out in the membership club Foundation Room. Celebrate an important event in one of our cool private party rooms and take home a special souvenir from our retail store. We look forward to welcoming you to our house!

our mission

To create a profitable, principled global entertainment company.
To celebrate the diversity and brotherhood of world culture.
To promote racial and spiritual harmony through love, peace, truth, righteousness and non-violence.

musical diversity

In our Music Halls, you will find almost every music genre imaginable. Rock n' Roll, Punk, Alternative, Heavy Metal, Rap, Country, Hip-Hop, Rhythm and Blues, Rock en Español, Jazz, Zydeco, Folk, Electronica and many other genres grace our stages. We welcome and celebrate music as a form of art and expression.

Music is a celebration. We design and manage venues with the complete experience in mind. *Best Outdoor Venue. Theatre of the Year. Arena/Auditorium of the Year. Best Large Outdoor Concert Venue. Best Live Music Club of the Year. Talent Buyer of the Year.* From large amphitheatres and arenas to small clubs, our venues and staff garner industry accolades year after year. View our upcoming shows, buy tickets and register for presales and special offers at www.hob.com.

The Gorge Amphitheatre is located in George, WA and has been voted Best Outdoor Arena several years running.

the visual blues

The House of Blues' walls feature American folk art affectionately referred to as the visual blues. With over a thousand original pieces of folk art, House of Blues houses one of the largest publicly displayed folk art collections in America. Like music, these pieces represent a form of artistic expression available to everyone.

philanthropy

Throughout our support of the International House of Blues Foundation (IHOBF), over 50,000 students and teachers experience the Blues SchoolHouse program in our music halls annually. This program explores the history, music and cultural impact of the blues and related folk art through live music, narration and a guided tour of our folk art collection. The program highlights African American cultural contributions and emphasizes the importance of personal expression. The IHOBF is dedicated to promoting cultural understanding and creative expression through music and art (www.ihobf.org).

House of Blues is the Home of Live Entertainment.

Have an intimate yet high energy experience at one of our many venues across the country.

Come visit us at one of our House of Blues Club venues where you can enjoy southern-inspired cuisine in our restaurant.

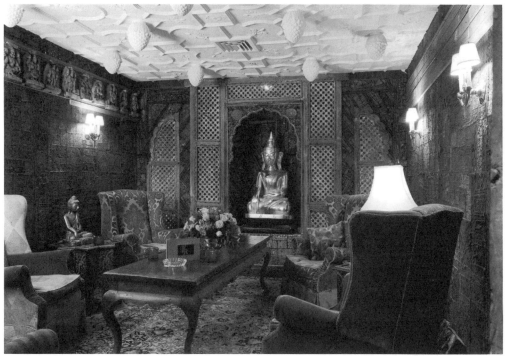

Experience an intimate fine dining, entertainment and lounge experience at the House of Blues Foundation Room.

T
A
B

T
A
B

T
A
B

T
A
B

T
A
B

T
A
B

Beginner Electric Guitar
CD Track List

BD = Bass and Drums on the track
BDR = Bass, Drums, and Rhythm Guitar on the track
BDRL = Bass, Drums, Rhythm Guitar and Lead on the track

1 - Introduction
2 – Parts of the Guitar
3 - Tuning/Names of the open strings
4 – Reading Chord Charts
5 – Your First Chords Am Em
6 – Basic Strumming Pattern Am Em
7 – Basic Strumming Pattern Am Em *BDR*
8 – Basic Strumming Pattern Am Em *BD*
9 – Major Open Chords
10 – Start Strumming E A D A
11 – Start Strumming E A D A *BDR*
12 – Start Strumming E A D A *BD*
13 – Picking Exercise
14 – Open Chord Rhythm/Alternate Strumming Am C Em G
15 – Open Chord Rhythm/Alternate Strumming Am C Em G *BDR*
16 - Open Chord Rhythm/Alternate Strumming Am C Em G *BD*
17 – Finger Exercise
18 – Basic Blues
19 – Basic Blues *BDR*
20 – Basic Blues BD
21 – Picking the Chords D G
22 – Picking the Chords D G *BDR*
23 – Picking the Chords D G *BD*
24 – Chromatic Scale
25 – Minor Open Chords Bm Cm Dm Fm Gm
26 – Minor Chord Progression
27 – Minor Chord Progression /Ghost Strum Am Dm G Em *BDR*
28 – Minor Chord Progression /Ghost Strum Am Dm G Em *BD*
29 – F Power Chord
30 – Bb Power Chord
31 – Power Chord Metal Rhythm
32 – Power Chord Metal Rhythm *BDR*
33 – Power Chord Metal Rhythm *BD*
34 – Minor Pentatonic Scale Key of A 1st Position
35 – Minor Pentatonic Scale Key of A 2nd Position
36 – Triplet Lead Pattern
37 – F Major Bar Chord
38 – F Minor Bar chord
39 – Drop D Tuning
40 – Drop D Metal Rhythm
41 – Drop D Metal Rhythm *BDR*
42 – Drop D Metal Rhythm *BD*
43 – Bb Major Bar Chord

Music Minus One Backing Tracks

Review Quiz Answer Key

1) C
2) C
3) B
4) A
5) C
6) C
7) A
8) C

FOR THE LATEST
CONCERT
CALENDARS

VISIT HOB.COM

HOUSE OF BLUES® members are always up to date, with the latest show information, announcements and **SPECIAL OFFERS**.

Membership is free, takes only 2 steps, and gives you access to all HOB.COM's services including:

- access to member-exclusive tickets through HOB Member Ticketing
- up-to-date information about House of Blues events in your area
- email notification of special offers and member-exclusive promotions
- eligibility to enter exclusive sweepstakes